FLAMINGO

by CAROLINE ARNOLD
photographs by RICHARD HEWETT

MORROW JUNIOR BOOKS · New York

PHOTO CREDITS: Permission to use the following photograph is gratefully acknowledged: Caroline Arnold, page 11.

The text type is 14 point Baskerville #2.

1 2 3 4 5 6 7 8 9 10

Library of Congress Cataloging-in-Publication Data. Arnold, Caroline. Flamingo / by Caroline Arnold : photographs by Richard Hewett.   p.   cm. Includes index. Summary: Examines the different kinds of flamingos, their physical characteristics, natural habitat, and behavior. ISBN 0-688-09411-2.—ISBN 0-688-09412-0 (lib. bdg.) 1. Flamingos—Juvenile literature. [1. Flamingos.] I. Hewett, Richard, ill.   II. Title. QL696.C56a76 1991 598.3′4—dc20 90-19186 CIP AC

Acknowledgments

Many people made it possible for us to do this book, and we would like to thank them for their time, expertise, and cheerful cooperation. We want to express our appreciation to all the people who helped us at Busch Gardens in Tampa, Florida, and particularly to Michael Wells, Curator of Birds, and to Glenda Gilmore and Christine Mackey in the Marketing Department. We are grateful for the assistance of Dennis Testa and his staff at Hialeah Racetrack, Hialeah, Florida. We also thank the Greater Los Angeles Zoo in Los Angeles, California, especially June Bottcher, Publicity; Michael Cunningham, Assistant Curator of Birds; and Cathy Christel, flamingo keeper. And, as always, we thank our editor, Andrea Curley, for her support and encouragement on this project.

A distant noise startled the group of flamingos feeding in the shallow water at the edge of the small lake. Suddenly all eyes were alert as the birds turned swiftly to move farther along the shore. Running as fast as he could go, four-week-old Chogogo raced to keep up with the long-legged adults. Like the bodies of other young flamingos, Chogogo's was still covered with soft, downy feathers. Although these would soon be replaced with longer, smooth feathers, it would be several years before the young flamingo wore the elegant, pink plumes of the older birds.

4

Chogogo was one of twenty-three flamingos newly hatched at Busch Gardens, a wild-animal park in Tampa, Florida. Each year, the flock has grown as new chicks have hatched. Now, with more than three hundred birds, it is one of the largest captive flocks of Caribbean flamingos in the world. Although most of the birds have grown up in captivity, the flamingos live and behave much like birds in the wild.

At the park, the flamingos are provided with shallow ponds for wading and feeding, open areas for resting, and an island for nest building. Once a day, keepers bring the flamingos food and check to make sure that all the birds are in good health.

Flamingos are one of the most popular exhibits at the park. Their brilliant feathers, spindly legs, snakelike necks, and unusual behavior make them easy to recognize and interesting to watch. No other wading bird is as tall as the flamingo, and few are so brightly colored.

7

In every country where flamingos live, people have their own name for them. The English word *flamingo* is the same as the Portuguese word. Like the common name for flamingos in many languages, it originally meant "red goose." Both flamingos and geese are large, long-necked birds and make similar loud, honking noises. Flamingos are not geese, but scientists believe both birds evolved from a common ancestor long ago. "Chogogo" is a South American Indian name for the flamingo and comes from a sound that flamingos make when they are feeding or flying.

Although there is some disagreement among scientists about how to classify the different kinds of flamingos, most agree that there are five species. All species of flamingos share the same general body shape and have similar behaviors, but they differ in size, color, and where they live.

Chogogo and the other flamingos in his group at Busch Gardens are Caribbean flamingos, also sometimes called American or West Indian flamingos. This kind of flamingo is found mainly on the islands and coastlines of the Caribbean. Occasionally a few birds wander as far as Bermuda and Brazil, and there is one group in the Galápagos Islands west of Ecuador. Although Spanish explorers discovered flamingos on the east coast of Florida in the 1500s, wild flamingos do not breed in the United States today. Those flamingos that are seen occasionally are believed to be birds that have escaped from captivity.

Adult Caribbean flamingos are the most brightly colored of all the flamingos. The depth of color varies from a light pink-orange to a deep coral, with the deepest red found on the bird's neck, breast, and wings. The flamingo's scientific name, *Phoenicopterus ruber ruber,* comes from Greek words meaning "crimson wing." As in other flamingos, the long feathers along the back edges of the wings are black. These sturdy flight feathers enable the bird to fly. The Caribbean flamingo has reddish purple legs and a bill that is yellow or light orange with a black tip.

The Caribbean flamingo is one of two subspecies of the greater flamingo, which is the largest species of flamingo and the kind most often exhibited in zoos. The African flamingo is the other subspecies, and it is found in southern Europe, Asia, and Africa. The main difference between the two subspecies is in the color of the adult birds. The African flamingo is mostly white or light pink with bright pink feathers only on the top of the wings. The flight feathers are black and the bill is pink, with a black tip.

The remaining four flamingo species are smaller, measuring from half to three-quarters of the body length of the greater flamingo. Like the African flamingo, they are mostly white or light pink. They include the lesser flamingo, which lives in Africa, and the Chilean, Andean, and James flamingos, which are found in South America. The James flamingo, first discovered in 1830 in Chile, was thought to be extinct for nearly one hundred years until another group was found in 1957. The Andean and James flamingos live in shallow lakes high in the Andes mountains.

African greater flamingos (left). Flamingos in Ngorongoro Crater, Tanzania (below).

Flamingos typically live in very large groups, or flocks, sometimes numbering more than a million birds. Usually we think of flamingos as living in lush, tropical gardens, but such an image is the opposite of the flamingos' usual natural home. Most wild flamingos live at the water's edge in remote, desolate areas where there are few large plants to provide shade and where the birds are constantly exposed to wind, sun, and weather. The remarkable thing about flamingos is how well adapted they are to this often harsh environment. In the tropics, flamingos must often endure extremely hot weather; those that live at high altitudes must be able to withstand cold temperatures as well.

Flamingos specialize in eating tiny plants and animals that grow only in water containing large amounts of salt

or soda. The shallow inland lakes and coastal lagoons where wild flamingos usually feed are located in areas of natural salt deposits or where evaporation contributes to a high level of salt in the water. Sometimes the salt concentration is nearly twice that of normal seawater. Some flamingos also live near the shallow water of alkaline lakes that form where there are natural soda deposits.

Few animals can tolerate drinking water with such a high mineral content, but, like other animals, flamingos need to drink water to live. Although they prefer pools of fresh rainwater if they are available, flamingos are also able to drink salty water. Special glands located underneath the flamingo's eyes remove excess salt from the body.

In a large group of flamingos, it is difficult to distinguish males and females because their coloring is the same. Usually males are slightly larger than females, with large Caribbean males growing more than 5 feet (1.5 meters) tall and weighing up to 8 pounds (3.6 kilograms). Female Caribbean flamingos are usually about 4½ to 5 feet (1.4 to 1.5 meters) tall and weigh about 6½ pounds (2.9 kilograms).

Although flamingos are able to reproduce at the age of three, males and females do not usually form pairs and produce chicks until they are about five years old. In captivity, flamingos often form pairs for life. Because it is difficult to do long-term studies of flamingos in the wild, scientists do not yet know if the wild birds form permanent pairs as well.

The breeding season for flamingos is in the spring and early summer, when there is sufficient food and enough rain to fill the shallow ponds around the nests. The exact times for the beginning and end of breeding depend on the weather and how far north or south the nesting ground is from the equator. As with many other birds, the flamingo's breeding cycle begins as days grow longer. In some years, if conditions are not just right, the birds may not breed at all. At zoos and animal parks in Florida, the breeding season for flamingos is usually March through July.

Caribbean flamingos: female (left), male (right).

15

Before flamingos build nests and lay eggs, they spend several months choosing mates. Although males usually start the courtship behaviors, both sexes take part in the displays. During this time they go through various movements that make them look as if they were performing parts of a giant seaside ballet. Courting flamingos seem to inspire one another, and you can usually see many birds exhibiting the same actions at the same time. Flamingos are highly social birds and do almost everything in groups.

In one kind of display called *head flagging,* several flamingos, mainly males, stand tall and sharply swing their heads from side to side. Head flagging is often followed by the *wing salute,* a movement in which a bird extends its wings for a moment and then snaps them closed. The *inverted wing salute* is similar except that the body is extended forward with the wings pointed down. In another typical courting movement, the flamingo loops its neck over its back and tucks its head under its wing for a moment. Perhaps the most amazing display is when a large group of flamingos suddenly starts walking as if marching to a silent drumbeat.

These displays may begin months before mating. It is not clear how the flamingos choose their mates, but as the courting process continues, pairs form and drop out of the group. They mate and begin to build their nest.

In the wild, flamingos use the same places to build their nests year after year. Nesting colonies of Caribbean flamingos are found on the Bahama Islands in the Caribbean, on the Yucatán peninsula in Mexico, on the island of Bonaire off the coast of Venezuela, and in the Galápagos Islands. At the end of the nesting season, the flamingos often disperse to other feeding sites.

Nesting colonies usually contain several hundred to several thousand nests, although occasionally a small colony has only fifty nests. During the nest-building period, there are frequent arguments between neighbors over the choice of nest sites. Flamingo pairs do not use the same nest each year and sometimes change nest sites several times in the course of building. Nests are usually built so close together that sitting birds can reach out to peck at their neighbors. Because flamingos nest only in groups, it is important for zoos and animal parks to have large flocks if they want the birds to breed. Even then, in order to breed successfully, the birds need a healthy diet, proper nesting sites, the right kind of nesting materials, and an enclosure where they feel secure.

Each spring at Busch Gardens, keepers bring in a special claylike mud and dump it at the edge of the lake near where the flamingos build their nests. Both male and female birds work on the nest, piling lumps of mud into a cone-shaped mound.

The flamingo reaches out, grabs a mouthful of mud, and deposits it at the edge of the nest site. Then it uses its flat, webbed feet to press the mud down into a shallow bowl. The finished nest is usually between 5 and 18 inches (12.8–46.2 centimeters) tall, although in cases where the same nest has been added to over several years, it can be up to 30 inches (76.9 centimeters) high. In the wild, if enough mud is not available, flamingos will build their nests with whatever they can find.

During the weeks they are building their nests, males and females mate periodically. Mating occurs in shallow water as the birds look for food. Then, when the nest is finished, the female lays a single white egg in the top of the nest. The egg is about 3½ inches (8.9 centimeters) long and 2 inches (5.1 centimeters) in diameter.

Because flamingos nest in such remote places, few people have ever seen flamingos nesting in the wild. For many years, people wondered what a flamingo did with its long legs when sitting on the nest. Now we know that, like other birds, a flamingo simply folds its legs to sit down. The middle joint, which looks as if it should be the flamingo's knee, is actually its ankle. That is why the leg appears to bend backward when it is moved. Like other birds, a flamingo stands on its toes.

Webbing between the toes helps the flamingo to paddle its feet while swimming.

The male and female flamingos take turns incubating their egg, that is, sitting on it to keep it moist and at an even temperature. Every few hours, the sitting bird stands up and uses its feet and bill to turn the egg. This prevents the developing chick from becoming stuck to the inside of the shell. Finally, after 28 to 31 days of incubation, the chick is ready to hatch.

The first sign of hatching is the appearance of a tiny hole in the shell. This opening, called the *pip*, is made when the chick presses against the shell with a hard knob on its bill. This small growth is called an *egg tooth*. It is not really a tooth and falls off soon after hatching. Over the next 24 to 36 hours, the chick twists and turns inside the shell as it works to break out. Finally the shell breaks open and the tiny chick emerges, its down feathers still matted to its body from the moisture inside the egg.

When Chogogo was newly hatched, he weighed about 3.2 ounces (91.4 grams) and was about 5 inches (12.8 centimeters) tall. Like all newly hatched flamingo chicks, he was so weak that he could barely stand. With his short legs and straight beak, he looked nothing like an adult flamingo, but more like a baby goose.

A young flamingo chick stays in the nest for only 5 to 8 days. Each day it grows bigger and stronger. At first it can stand for just a few minutes at a time. By the second or third day, its legs are strong enough for it to walk around the top of the nest when its parent stands up. When the parent bird sits down on the nest again, the baby bird snuggles underneath.

When their chick is in the nest, the parent flamingos guard it closely and snap at any other flamingo that comes too near. The parents are also watchful for predators such as hawks, eagles, or sea gulls that might attack their baby. Because of their size, adult flamingos have few natural predators other than humans. In the Bahamas, they are occasionally killed by domestic pigs that have become wild.

By his fourth or fifth day, Chogogo was able to sit on the side of the nest and poke his head out from under his parent's wing. There he was safe but could see what was going on in the rest of the flamingo colony.

When Chogogo was about a week old, he was ready to leave the nest for the first time. While his parents watched, he carefully climbed down the side of the nest to the edge of the water below. Already his sturdy legs had begun to turn from orange to the black color of the older chicks. His bill was also darkening and beginning to turn slightly downward. Like the other flamingo chicks, he was able to swim if the water became too deep for him to walk on the bottom of the lake.

Once out of the nest, Chogogo returned to it occasionally for the next few days. At first his parents guarded him carefully and shooed away any larger birds that came too near. However, as Chogogo grew bigger and stronger, he spent more time on his own. Soon he left the nest permanently and joined a group of other chicks close to his age. One of the older flamingos often acted as a baby-sitter and watched over the youngsters. These young birds would remain together for the next few months as they learned to fend for themselves. Although the chicks could pick up small bits of food with their bills, they continued to beg food from their parents as well.

From the time a flamingo chick is hatched, its parents feed it *crop milk*, a nutritious liquid that is formed in the throat of adult birds. When Chogogo became hungry, he called out until one of his parents heard him. Each flamingo has its own distinctive call, and even in groups of many birds, parents and chicks quickly learn to recognize each other's call.

To get food, a chick stretches its neck upward toward the parent's bill. The parent bird feeds its youngster by allowing the crop milk to drip from the end of its bill into the younger bird's mouth. A newly hatched chick is fed every 45 to 90 minutes, day and night. A flamingo chick grows rapidly, and as it becomes older, feeding becomes less frequent. Parents usually feed their youngster until it is four to five weeks old. A flamingo chick cannot get enough food on its own until its bill curves downward so that it can feed with its head upside down like the adult flamingos.

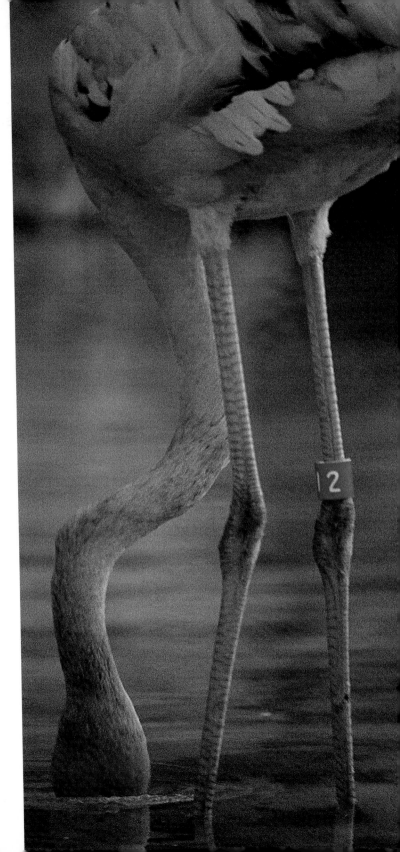

Although flamingos sometimes use their bills to pick up pieces of food, they usually eat by filtering tiny organisms out of the water. The flamingo's bill is one of its most unusual features. Unlike the bills of most birds, it is hinged on the upper part rather than the lower. This allows the flamingo to open and close its bill easily while moving forward with its head upside down. The edges of the bill are lined with stiff, comblike bristles called *lamellae*. These act like small sieves when the mouth is closed.

To eat, the flamingo walks slowly through a lake or lagoon and uses its long, slender neck to lower its head to the water's surface in order to scoop food and water into its mouth. With its head still upside down, the flamingo uses its large, fleshy tongue to push the water out through the bristles. Food particles are trapped on the inside of the flamingo's mouth. Then they are removed by the tongue and swallowed. A feeding flamingo sometimes moves in a circular pattern and uses its feet to stir up food from the bottom. Flamingos also feed in deep water, tipping their tails up as ducks, geese, and swans do and submerging their heads to look for food.

At zoos and wildlife parks, foods for flamingos include vegetables, grains, fish meal, nutritious pellets, and vitamin and mineral supplements. In the wild, flamingos eat what grows in the areas where they live. In some places, the main food is insect larvae. In others, the flamingos eat small clams, brine shrimp, aquatic insects, seeds, and small fish. Almost everywhere, one of the most important foods for flamingos is the algae that grow on the mud at the bottom of their lagoons. The algae themselves are nutritious, and they also trap tiny one-celled animals, worms, insects, and other small organisms.

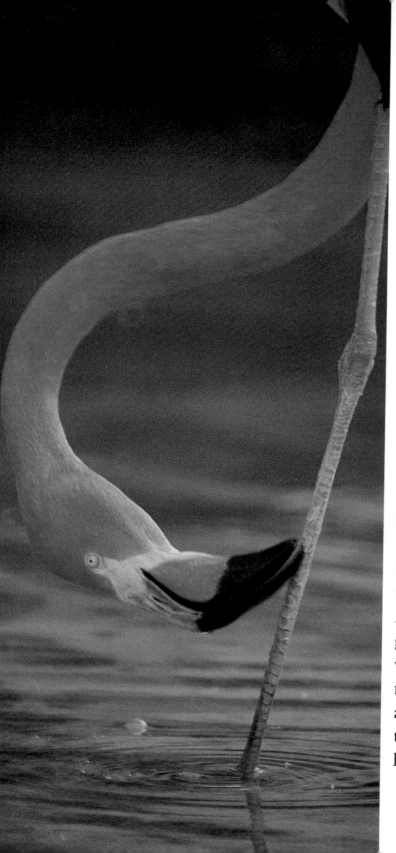

Some of the most important elements in a flamingo's diet are substances called carotenoids. These yellow, orange, or red molecules are produced by green plants, fungi, and bacteria. When animals eat foods that have carotenoids in them, their bodies change these substances into other forms. Many animals, including humans, change carotenoids into vitamin A, which then helps the animal to see, grow, and reproduce. Flamingos convert carotenoids into the pigments that make their feathers so colorful. Large amounts of carotenoids are found in the natural diet of flamingos, particularly in the algae they eat.

Until the 1950s, when the effect of carotenoids on body color in flamingos was first studied, zoos had been mystified by why their flamingos lost the beautiful red coloring in their feathers after they had been in captivity for a while. It was because their foods did not have enough carotenoids in them. Now zoos and animal parks make sure that flamingos have enough of this important substance. Carotenoids are present in the ground-up beets or carrots the flamingos are fed, or added as a chemical supplement to the flamingos' food.

In the park, as in the wild, the flamingos alternate periods of eating with periods of resting. Perhaps one of the most typical views of a flamingo is a bird perched on one stiff leg, sound asleep, with its head tucked under its wing. Flamingos develop a good sense of balance early in life and can remain on one leg for a long time.

When Chogogo and the other flamingos were not eating or resting, they were often preening, that is, using their bills to clean and arrange their feathers. Feathers protect the flamingos' skin and help keep the birds warm and dry. Preening helps to spread body oil over the feathers to make them waterproof. Flamingos become wet while feeding and also during rainstorms, which occur often in the tropics. (Adult birds that are incubating eggs remain on their nests when it is raining to prevent the bowl-shaped top of the nest from filling with water.)

At four and a half weeks of age, Chogogo's legs were much stronger and longer than when he hatched. Their color had changed to solid black, and his light-colored down had been replaced with a coat of much darker gray.

When Chogogo was five weeks old, longer, smooth feathers grew in over the down. Except for black feathers on the wings, the first juvenile feathers of a young flamingo are a grayish brown, with a slight tinge of pink.

When Chogogo and the other young flamingos reach seven months of age, they will be about half the size of adult birds. At this point their juvenile feathers will fall out and be replaced by new, mostly pink ones. This process is called molting. Molting occurs gradually, with just a few feathers coming out at a time. They are quickly replaced with new feathers. Like adult flamingos, the young birds will continue to molt once a year. Each time they molt, they will look more like adult birds. Two-, three-, and four-year-old flamingos can be distinguished from full-grown adults because their legs are still dark and they often retain some gray feathers on the back of the neck.

Although young flamingos begin to exercise their wings while still in the nest, they cannot actually fly until their long flight feathers have completely grown in. This occurs when they are three to three and a half months old. At most zoos and animal parks, keepers clip the wing feathers of young birds when they are a few days old. This does not hurt them but does help to prevent the birds from flying away.

41

In the United States, the only large group of free-flying flamingos lives in a sanctuary in the center of the Hialeah Racetrack in Florida. This flock, which began in the 1930s with twenty-five imported birds, now numbers more than six hundred. Although the birds fly away occasionally for short periods, they always return to their nesting sites and source of food.

To take off, a flamingo runs as fast as it can and at the same time flaps its wings rapidly. Once it is airborne, the large wings lift the bird easily into the sky and propel the flamingo swiftly forward. In the air, a flamingo is one of the most graceful birds alive. Few sights are more impressive than a group of these huge black-and-pink birds circling overhead. Because they fly with their legs extended and their necks stretched forward, they look like large flying crosses. In flight, as on the ground, the birds call out to one another and sound something like a flock of geese. Flamingos can land on either land or water, using their feet as brakes to stop themselves.

You can see flamingos at many zoos and wildlife parks in the United States and Canada. In the safety of captivity, flamingos like Chogogo can look forward to a long life. No one is sure how long flamingos live in the wild, but in zoos they have lived more than forty years and may be able to live even longer than that. Numbered bands around the legs of flamingos often help people identify individual birds and monitor their age, health, and activities.

Zoos and animal parks that breed flamingos are helping us to understand their behavior and how they grow. Captive-bred birds also provide a supply of flamingos for other zoos. This makes it less necessary to take birds from the wild for zoo exhibits. Although flamingos still exist in large numbers in the wild, they are becoming threatened as civilization moves closer to their traditional breeding sites. The single greatest danger to wild animals today is the disappearance of their natural habitat as people develop it for commercial and recreational uses. Flamingos are particularly sensitive to disturbances, and when people come too close to their nesting areas, the flamingos leave, sometimes abandoning the site altogether. There are only a few places that make suitable breeding grounds for flamingos, so when the flamingos are forced off these, they have almost nowhere else to go.

Index